THE DREAM-HOUSE

By the same author

POEMS
The Rain-Giver
The Battle of Maldon and other Old English Poems
    (translations)
Beowulf *(translation)*

TRAVEL
Pieces of Land: Journeys to Eight Islands

FOR CHILDREN
The Callow Pit Coffer
The Earth-Father
The Fire-Brother
Green Blades Rising:
    a Cultural History of the Anglo-Saxons
The Green Children
Havelok the Dane
King Horn
The Pedlar of Swaffham
The Sea Stranger
Storm and Other Old English Riddles
The Wildman
Wordhoard *(with Jill Paton Walsh)*

AS EDITOR
New Poetry 2 (The Arts Council)
Running to Paradise:
    an Introductory Selection of the Poems of W. B. Yeats
Winter's Tales 14
Winter's Tales for Children 3

THE DREAM-HOUSE

Poems by

Kevin Crossley-Holland

ANDRE DEUTSCH

First published 1976 by
André Deutsch Limited
105 Great Russell Street London WC1

Printed in Great Britain by
A. Wheaton & Co Exeter

ISBN 0 233 96805 9

for Ruth

Do you listen for the nightingale? Lady
of compassion, Lady of contrition; Mrs
Gaskell's orphan.

Part thorn, part city, just a trick with
a lisp, you embody a million causes. You
lie in truth.

Gleaner in a field after the reapers;
from you Jesse stemmed; Lady of such
harvests.

Acknowledgments

Thanks are due and gladly given to the editors of the
following publications in which some of these poems were
first printed: Cornhill, The New Review, New Statesman,
Outposts, *PEN Anthology 1974* and *PEN Anthology 1975*,
Poetry and Audience, *Poetry Book Society Christmas
Supplement*, The Scotsman, The Sunday Times, Tablet,
The Times Literary Supplement, Wave, The Poetry Review.

'The First Island,' 'The Dream-House', 'Props' and 'Bede's
Death-Song' first appeared in *Pieces of Land,* published
by Victor Gollancz.

'More than I Am' has been illustrated by Ralph Steadman
and printed as Broadsheet No. 5 by the Steam Press.

'The Dream-House', illustrated with a wood engraving by
Angela Lemaire, was Keepsake Poem No. 2 (entitled 'The
Wake') printed by the Keepsake Press. It was read on
Dial-a-Poem which is sponsored by the Greater London Arts
Association.

'Restless Ones' was commissioned by the Ilkley Literature
Festival as part of a tribute to W. H. Auden and was printed
in facsimile by the Scolar Press.

Seven of the poems in Section II have appeared from the
Sceptre Press under the title *Petal and Stone*.

'Vision' has been printed as an Arts Council card.

'Hills' was broadcast on Poetry Now, Radio 3.

Contents

I

Hills

1.

No little people come out of that hill.
It is a gaunt grey whale,
Taking light, killing it, offering nothing.

Each spring it is disappointed
By its own sterility:
No grass, no life amongst the grass.

What has gone wrong?
Its head is in the clouds
Wondering what the magic words are.

2.

Old wives say:
Stay put where you were born –
At the foot of a slagheap or in a green valley –
And you will suffer no harm

In limb or in liver or lung.
I seem as sound as any
And yet I am out of tune
And come and shout, 'Where are they?'

Where are they? Where are they?
My words return
From the Hill.

3.

Those are my hills:
Beyond the dawn-ash fields,
The placable dark breathing bulks
In motionless stances,
Beyond the elms that stand like sentinels,
Those are my hills
With many rooms I entered.

4.

At my feet the map,
The colours growing light corrects,
So utterly familiar that I can tell
Each item added, all that has been lost.
At my head the rise, the ridge, quite patient,
And all the beeches still night-blurred.
A bird mutters on a branch.

O
I am growing into the ground again.

Fortification

for Barry and Maggie

Gat-toothed grey hill.
                    Another encampment,
Another whorl of escarpments, bulging
And vital.
            Eyes at the interstices,
Regular, round as compasses and clocks;
And behind ramparts, hidden from without,
Orderly mounds of slingstones, small forests
Of ash-spears, sunstruck shields and bodyguards,
All the gear, ready.
                    Within the enclosure
A mill of herded humans and livestock,
A concourse with no air of business
As usual, wholly abandoned.
                        They pound
The fort's last grassblade flat, voluntary
Prisoners in their own windy village,
Settled on their hidebound plans, old and young
With horses and cattle, pigs, hens.
                                Distance,
Middle distance, blur and definite small
Knots dislocate from the tangle, make off
And hole up in their huts.
                        Squalls, grunts and shouts
Begin to sound singular, the last out
Hurry as if they have to.
                    Enter night
From all sides, a sudden flurry of wind
Like the wind of the dead rustles and leaves
The arena empty.

                    I could no more
Ignore the challenge here than journey close
To my birthplace and ignore it; I have
A white handkerchief, a quiver of needs
I cannot flight.
          Climber in the blue hour
To the contour of an answer.
                         Wanting
Further admission, a password-seeker,
Poking round, following lines of small hills
Moles have thrown up, and shortly before dark
Emerging from the compound, both pockets
Stuffed with sherds.
                  Nothing sharply specified,
But in some way reassured, half-defined,
Apprehending again there may never
Be clear questions, pointed, but simply this
Returning need settled by communion:

Traveller, peaceable, until the next bend.

In the Company of Saints

It was my only meeting with that man.
Glad of his van's noise that half-justified
Our silences, we jolted out of Cleggan
And, under the banked and glaring sky,

Bruised across miles of rubbed sand to Omey.
We stumbled through deep dunes there, immense shoals
That shift entirely when Malin's under siege,
And came as if by chance to an incorrupt hollow.

The latest storms had resurrected at our feet
Pink keystones and the tops of walls – the church
Of a small saint unmentioned in dictionaries
And Calendars. The bright light pronounced

Each granite block a perfect fit, the gable-ends
Truly cut, unmarred in a millennium.
The place looked almost ready for service,
As if at any moment we would hear

Fechin and his monks singing God's praises,
Recrossing the spit. Conscious of years shared,
The generous experience of that sanctuary,
We settled on one bank. But then that man

Swiftly turned the talk from wonder, told me
Of double death – our friend and her daughter.
With such care he chose the time, the place
Which partly transmuted that horror into myth.

Their lives and deaths seemed one with ours;
Kneeling there is the company of saints, it seemed
We could contain and ride and redeem them: a shock
Immediate yet at once remote, as it is now.

14

The First Island

There it was, the island.

Low-slung sandhills like land-waves, fettered by marram.
One hut, a dark nugget. Across the creeks gleaming like
tin, like obsidian, across the marshes almost rust,
olive, serge, fawn, purpled for a season, the island.

We shoaled on the Staithe, stared out and possessed it;
children who collar half the world with a shout, and
share it in a secret.

Old men sat on a form lodged against the wall.
Of course we did not ask. We knew. They were too old.

There it was, and at times not there. Atmosphere
thickened, earth and air and water became one lung;
we were in a wilderness.

In a coat of changing colours it awaited us. In the
calm seas of our sleep it always loomed, always ahead.
We woke, instantly awake. As if we never had been
tired, and all things were possible.

So the boat came for us. The island stretched out to
us and we took it for granted. And no one asked by
which creeks we had come or could return.

Man's Company

The man turned from the hopeless hollow
Before the breaking wave
And the harsh grief of the shingle
That cannot help itself.

He crossed sun-crazed mud's mosaic,
Then passed between dunes,
And found again the winding path
To follow far inland.

Late, he settled in a springfield
Chaperoned by finches;
The daylong cirrhus
Dissolved above his head.

Ears for the fresh susurrus, susurrus;
Eyes for the silken grass,
Gathering, rippling like water:
He dreamed once more of woman.

The Chinar

translated from the Georgian of Nikoloz Baratashvili,
1817–1845

In a desolate place, precipitous, a young chinar stands,
Long-limbed and spacious and graceful; its leaves are
      ten thousand hands.
Daydream in its deep shadow, half listen to those
      rustling leaves
And the laughing river, unpick the web of trouble this
      world weaves.

The Mtkvari murmurs, and the swaying chinar whispers,
      whispers,
Soporific sounds fathering a first dream, then sweet
      sisters.
I believe things inanimate have a language of their own
More immediate than any tongue the world knows, or has
      known.

The Mtkvari, like a lover at the feet of his proud mistress,
Longs to clasp the tree's roots, and it surges up the
      precipice,
Dashes itself on the dark cliff. But the chinar, disdainful,
Shakes its head as if such court was not pleasurable
      but painful.

Whenever the wind enters and moves the tree, the water
      sighs
More deeply, as though from jealousy; the waves gather
      and rise
And break on rock. In this way, secretly, man is torn
      apart
Over and again if passion's furnace rages in his heart.

Exposure

Local Romeo taps twice on a pipe,
somewhere over there, beyond the lilac
in the darkness, which one of those terraced
houses I can never tell.
                    Net curtains
part perhaps, so flimsy it may be wind,
just a manoeuvre, or the eye's failure
to separate blacknesses. Does he climb
now, does she come, how do they manage it
in such utter quietness?
                    On Shooters Hill
the distant cars move on unknown journeys,
comforting, almost, as the house, maybe,
creaks in the way old houses do, and in
the garden there are whispers.
                    So they lie,
probably, truth-telling now, now all things
to each other, in a sort of hemmed peace,
a sweet ring of undefended silence,
risky as any human paradise.

More than I am

He enters her,
Their world's Pacific, compact as an egg.

Each breathes 'I am more than I am',
In this small room, on this creaking bed.

All that has been is absolved
And what will be is contained

In this intermittent love-war;

This is time's only meaning here,
Hours pass outside the door.

Again, again he enters her.
She cries, and will not have it otherwise.

He seems a giant now astride her,
Bent only on re-entering her,

Begging to be reborn.

Sleepsong

No dreams of good or ill
seem now to prove you;
you lie utterly still.
I do not move you

as I carefully move:
no hitch in your breath,
no eyelid flicker. Love,
rest, I shall keep faith

with you. Sleep always so
now. At last the time
for carelessness to grow
from chime, chime to chime.

Rapids

1.

'Of course I will not go. I will be here.
Of course I'll still be here, I promise you.'
It is enough, I can still reassure
Them with words true now, not for tomorrow.
So they go off for conkers, shout, and fire
For unripe high-fliers; they break a bough . . .

What is there we do not wound with our touch?
My two sons, I cannot love you too much.

2.

All afternoon he talked about that bridge
Through Salisbury, Stockbridge, Basingstoke and Staines.
The pressure of things we did not manage,
Tears suppressed, issues skirted like towns . . .
We reached peeling London, parted, climbed, dodged
Pedestrians like unexploded mines,

Ran back towards each other. It was his cue.
'Can't you stay tonight? Please stay. Why must you . . .

3.

Don't keep asking. Let him open the door.
He is entitled to his privacy.
Isn't it enough for him to endure
This going, is it so necessary
To thrash it all out? No, he must first dare
Himself, the rapids of his misery.

This is a test of love. Leave him alone.
He is not mine, or hers; he is his own.

The Burning Bush

Behold, the bush burned with fire,
and the bush was not consumed.
Do not think that fierce desire,
consummate, can be resumed

for a further blazing season.
Every twig burst into flame
petals, light coursed through each vein
and the heart asked no reason.

Once more its leaves were ashen
green: the bush stood with no show,
but having suffered passion,
stood apart, contained, and glowed.

The Happy Land

The first lines of 'The Phoenix', translated from Old English
for Georgina Hammick

I have heard that far from here,
away to the east, is a place without equal,
rightly renowned. Few men reach
that remote region of this middle-earth,
for through God's might it is removed
from sinners. That land is so lovely, endowed
with delights, earth's sweetest scents.
It is an unique, inland island; noble,
unshakeable the Shaper of that country!
Voices in harmony, the door of heaven,
are disclosed often to happy men there.
That is a festive land, full of forests,
spacious under the skies. Neither rain nor snow,
frost-breath nor fire-blast,
hail-flail nor rime-fall,
neither warm weather nor winter sleet
can work the least harm there, but the plain
is inviolate, utterly perfect. That fine land
is alight with flowers. Neither alp nor fell
sheer steeply there, no rugged escarpments
climb to the clouds, as they do here;
there are no valleys, gorges, gloomy hill-caves,
no hills or ridges – nothing uneven
has any place there, but the great plain
spreads out below heaven, fertile and flourishing.
In their writings wise men say
that fair field is twelve fathoms
higher than any of the mountains in our country
that soar, shining, under the stars.
That peerless place lies at peace: gleaming
the sun-sharp glades, serene the forest.
Ripe fruit does not fall, the trees stand
green in all seasons, as God bade them.

In summer and winter alike, orchards
are laden with fruit: the fluttering leaves
will not wither, fire will not scathe them,
until a change afflicts the world entire. . . .

II

Clean Monday, Ramnous

A fallen streamer rustles and sidles
Across the floor. After each guest and gust
The door slams; a youngest daughter bridles
At some strange hungry smile, and in the dust

Outside, the hens scatter at the clatter
To the rough yard's corners, nettles, the fence.
Their loss is that nothing does not matter:
Assiduous devotees of nonsense,

They peck at grit and small chips of marble
And ignore the field's red lips across the road
Where the man waits. The swirling winds garble
His shouts, translate them into ode, then goad.

His girl hears, rises; again the door slams.
He carries a kite - an eagle or buzzard.
With skill he hoists it, plays it, now it runs
And climbs further before blast and blizzard.

Then his daughter takes it. When it tugs, dives,
She shrieks with such excited fear, aware
Of ravening beyond her, and of lives
She could live that have not yet escaped her.

So she yields, he resumes. Hand over hand
He holds the line just as he grasps his spade.
This one day he abandons the land;
He forgets the vine, the growing green blade,

His taverna's patrons, already tight.
He is washing off the soil of the year,
Acknowledging Lachesis. The great kite
Is like a tongue preying on air, a prayer.

Petal and Stone

An old antithesis: petal and stone.
There were anenomes near that valley site,
Furled against such freezing wind. They alone
Looked living in that mottled place – blood-bright.

She dropped to her knees by a brilliant small
Colony, carefully selected one,
And leaned back against a rock. That was all
It seemed, but it could have been a lion:

Only the torso, and that mauled by time,
But still the defiant cold lord of the land.
She stretched out against it, so tender, feline:
The flower had opened to wilt in her hand.

Tenacious Offspring

Few finds on those slopes –
a grasp of coarseware, part of an unremarkable rim:
something like the wind had swept them clean
down to the sea, almost every sherd
and marble chipping, leaving only bulky
Penetelic slabs.
        Yet there, amongst scrub,
under the scoured and fretted temple,
were scarlet, saffron, copper, tenacious offspring,
the first wild flowers. While the wind
rifled, you picked just a handful,
brilliant spirit in a stoup of flesh and bone.

A Guided Tour

Oranges and lemons,
says la belle Miranda,
lady of such wonders.
Self evident! Our guide
is very thorough
at our expense,
and offers us no apples.
Marble quarry . . . Defile . . .
Ladies and gentlemen,
there is an old legend . . .
Yes, but almond blossom
also, electric wild iris,
everywhere such promises.
Oranges . . . Lemons . . .
I stare out at the groves
and remember that magic tree,
golden nutmeg, silver pear.
All these fruit look
as if someone had reached up
and, parting the branches,
one by one, with care,
lovingly fastened
or painted them there.

At Mycenae

The marble still bleeds, Clytemnestra.
Blame Homer.
If only historians and epic poets
Would also record the unspectacular.
Sheep bleat amongst the scrub
On the hillside opposite.
The lives of shepherds
Were not affected seriously at the time,
And time barely touches them.
Now the sheep move on their runs
And a light wind carries
To the stillness of the palace
A sweet wash once more
Of distant, ordinary bells.

Behind Him

The old man peered into the mirror:
He saw the poppies there and picked them.
He peered into the mirror,
He knew there was something just behind him
If only he could fathom it.
He turned round; that was no good.
The old man peered into the mirror:
Sweet crushed cradling grass,
Green light white between the leaves
Of elm trees tall and toppling.
The old man raised his arms
But he knew there was something else.
He turned round; that was no good.
A pool of still water he bathed his hands in,
Mist rising and falling, falling,
A sea of blind iris.

History

We are hosts to the living dead.
They are neither for us nor against us.
They couldn't care less. Drink; eat.
What does tomorrow mean to a child?

Apologia

You thought it was not good enough
to write finely-wrought verses
about archaeological remains
and cited Brecht: *What times are these
when it is almost a crime to talk
about trees because it implies
silence about so many atrocities?*
You are passionate but humourless.
Not all poets need or even should
redeem the squalid deals
of politicians by pleading
common causes, rights, denominators.
There are such world wonders: even today
regular irregular flint-grey waves
under the tower, the first lamb there
amongst stones and discoloured bones.
There are so many languages
for our recurring crises,
and many great poems penned by men
who didn't give a damn for politics.
You are so arrogant.
What leads you to suppose
we can do with less of such hopeful diversity,
or even that we have different intentions?

T.D.H.—B

III

A Way of Life

The boat berths from Magheroarty Pier.
The crew turn their backs
To stain the jetty wall.

Age has decayed the round tower,
One-eyed like evil Balor.
Debris plugs it.

Lumpish grey objects
Deter the soiled water
In the open drains at West Town.

The turf from Tormore makes poor burning.
The fire needs stirring
Without sods brought in from the mainland.

A hen clucks in Connor's cottage
Over its dead sister.
The mongrel squirms with chicken fleas.

O'Brien's top blanket
Sweats with his body's heat:
At dawn a rash of water globules.

Fish heads flung from boats
At Camusmore.
The cat deposits one on the doorstep.

Nobody empties
The Elsan backing the knacker's yard.
The wind is blowing the wrong way.

A chain of washing dances on a rope
tied round the gashed torso
Of the Tau-cross.

A rusting green van lies shattered
On rock, shoved over the edge
Of Columcille's hole.

Stubble on the chin,
Brilliant devious eyes behind Keogh's counter.
Studied calm: distilled poteen.

They made Kelly's coffin themselves,
Cursing the storm, gazing at the mainland.
It is not airtight.

'No rats here.'
Dhugan lifts the deterrent island clay
And presents it to an incredulous visitor.

A splinter of blue stands over Muckish,
A morning rainbow over still water.
Nobody has risen.

Shadows

A rib of shadow on the marsh,
It grows like a dark thought;

My skull begins to gather
All the far-off booming of the sea.

A crab's skeleton disintegrates
Between my careful fingers

And the salt harvest where I stand
Gleams like guttering candle-ends.

O most loved when almost lost,
This most uncommon common place,

Still at dusk mysterious,
My sea-threatened wilderness . . .

The dark wave sweeps through me.
A rib of shadow on the marsh.

Props

translated from the Irish of Máirtín O Direáin

Give no ground, soul.
Grasp all that ever mattered.
Don't quail like some bearded boy
Because your friends have failed you.

You have seen a sandpiper often enough,
Lonely on a shining rock;
The wave yielded nothing
And yet it did not blame him.

You did not come
With the cap of happiness,
But guardians were placed
Around your wooden cradle.

Poor guardians they were:
Iron tongs hanging over you,
A piece of your father's clothing,
Poker in the fire.

Lean on your props
Against slow tide and neap tide;
Keep in the spark of your dream,
To betray that is death.

The caul enveloping the head, in Irish literally 'the cap of happiness', is traditionally considered to be a sign of good luck, and a preservative against drowning.

The Dream-House

My eyes are sore. They sting with my own salt.
This day I have been the fetch of the sea.

Those shapes are round and kind yet fast as rocks.
What are their names? I must think of their names.

They speak firm words in soft ways. I like it
When they speak, and when they sit with no words.

Look at him, then. Look at him. John, John, John,
Once more a small wee boy, old bag of bones.

At your head the wax burns and Christ stares down
From the Cross. It is all just as it was

When you were a child and I was a child,
Each on our own in the long dark. You seem

To sleep as I would. No, it is not that,
Or it is that but more than that. I look

And you are not tired and not sad; you are calm
As the swell of the slow deep sea in June.

All you were in your time smiles as you meet,
Like a long lost friend, the end of all time.

First James now John in six months. So I am
The last one. Soon he must leave his clean sheets,

His bed, for the press of earth on the lid.
What are these? Why do I cry tears once more?

My sleeve is as rough as a tom cat's tongue.
Do not look at me. I am troughs and waves.

What is that noise? That noise? A gale of laughs
From young men and girls that sit at the hearth.

Where do they think they are? This is a wake,
Not a dance hall. They grin and nudge and wink.

John, John, John, this is your wake. I will stand
When I can and throw the pack of them out.

This is your wake, not a dance hall. No, no,
I am wrong. Let it be as it should be.

Let there be smoke from pipes, the games and songs.
They are his friends who chose to come and choose

To stay as long as this long night. We were
The same, quick in our words and ways, our blood.

What is the time? The priest will come with prayers,
Then the day with wind, tears. It will be done.

Your will be done. John, John, John, I will clean
The lamp in your room as if you were here.

Bede's Death Song

translated from Old English

Before he leaves on his fated journey
No man will be so wise that he need not
Reflect while time still remains
Whether his soul will win delight
Or darkness after his death-day.

The Fortunes of Men

translated from Old English

Often and again, through God's grace,
man and woman usher a child
into the world and clothe him in gay colours;
they cherish him, teach him as the seasons turn
until his young bones strengthen,
his limbs lengthen. So his father and mother
first carry him, then walk with him,
and lavish gifts and garments on him. Only God
know how years will use the growing man.

One will die young, afflicting
his family. The wolf, the grey heath-stalker,
will gorge on him; then his mother will mourn.
Man cannot control his fortune.

Hunger will devour one, storm dismast another,
one will be spear-slain, one hacked down in battle.
One will enjoy life without seeing light,
he will grope about; one with feeble sinews,
a crippled foot, will curse at the pain,
rankled and resentful he will fret at fate.

One will drop, wingless, from the high tree
in the wood; look how he flies still,
jolts through the air, until the branches
fail him. Then sadly he slumps
by the trunk, robbed of life; he falls
to earth and his soul flies from him.

One will have no choice but to chance
remote roads, to carry his own food
and leave dew tracks amongst foreign people
in a dangerous land; he will find few
prepared to entertain him; the exile
is shunned everywhere because of his bad history.

One will swing from the tall gallows,
sway in death, until his bloodmasked body,
casket of his soul, has been violated.
There the raven pecks out his eyes,
the dark bird rips his corpse to pieces;
and he cannot thwart the vile thief's
intrusion with his hands, for his life is ended;
flayed, forsaken, pale on the tree,
he endures his fate, shrouded in swirling
death-mist. Men spit at his name.

One will suffer agony on the pyre,
seething fire will swallow the fated man;
death will claim him quickly there,
the cruel red flames; that woman keens
who sees those tongues swathe her son.

The sword's edge will shear one sitting
at the mead-bench, some angry man soaked
with beer or wine. His words were too hasty.
One will not stay the cupbearer's hand
until he is befuddled; then at the feast
he cannot keep his tongue or his temper
but most meanly forfeits his life;
he suffers death, severance from joys;
and men style him a self-slayer,
and grieve the indulgence of that drunkard.

One, by God's grace, will overcome
all the hardships that bedevilled his youth
and achieve happiness in old age;
he will welcome the rising sun, and receive
riches, treasures and the mead-cup from his people –
as much as anyone can own in this life.

So mighty God apportions his lot
to each man on this middle-earth.
He grants, allocates, ordains fate:
for one happiness, hardship for another;
for one a young man's ecstasy, success for another
in savage swordplay; for one strength in wrestling,
for one skill in boxing and fame for bravery,
fortune for one at dice, a devious mind
for chess. Some scribes become wise.
The goldsmith fashions a marvellous gift for one;
many times that man tempers and decorates
for the great king, who grants him broad acres
in return. He readily accepts them.

One will delight a gathering, gladden
men sitting at the mead-bench over their beer;
the joy of the bibbers is redoubled there.
He will settle beside his harp
at his lord's feet, and be handed treasures;
he is always prepared to pluck strings
with a plectrum – with that hard, hopping thing
he creates harmonies. Harpist, heart's desire!

One will tame that arrogant wild bird,
the hawk on the fist, until the falcon
becomes gentle; he puts jesses on it
and feeds it still in fetters; he weakens
the swift peregrine, so proud of its plumage,
with mere morsels until that bird, servile
in garment and in flight, obeys its sustainer,
is trained to the hand of the young warrior.

In these wondrous ways the Guardian of Hosts
has shaped and assigned the fortunes of men
on this middle-earth, and ordained the estate
of every man and woman in this world.
Wherefore let us all thank Him,
that He, in His mercy, cares for men.

A Little Faith at Brattahlid

The seagulls scream like children and all is not well.

Uneasily the ashen swell humps and subsides;
if only crests would unsheath, and tonight assuage.

On the dun strand lie wasted ribs, west over sea
There is no blood. Even my Magnus shakes his head

Over the question nobody asks, I can see
He sets no store now on a boat before next spring,

And thinks us more thwarted because of our high hopes
And idle talk of third summer lucky. Next spring!

What would they find? A scatter of pecked, unburied
Bones. I say it is bad to be ignored, and worse

To be forgotten, worst of all to accept it
With vacant eyes and shoulder-shrugs, such self-defeat.

This is an outrage. Who is so mean that fury
Does not flare in him? Count how many can still stand.

Here is wood enough. Here are saw, hammer, adze,
If only we have strength to take them in our hands.

Christ and Balder both be damned. I would rather sink
In a leaky boat than pray for my salvation,

Each day weaker, waiting, hungry, anxious, bitter,
Then found later spreadeagled in this rotten hut.

I can see no one trying to walk on water.

Restless Ones

'Doom is dark and deeper than any sea-dingle.'
- W. H. Auden

Creek fills, light fails.
Yellowed pewter and faded pink
And blue, blue. A buoy withstands
The swirl; skirl of unseen wings.

By night they come unkempt to concrete
And lichen airfields long untenanted,
Outcasts, exile and self-exile,
Scarecrows in soft parishes
Wind visits and welfare men
Visit, viewing sodden furrows
With little surprise, poor resignation,
Clothes flapping, unable to fly,
Stayed by the sea, its cruel silver
And gold chains, what choice?
Fate leaves little freedom.

Colours fail, phosphorescent water
Slacks; tide turns, tugs.

Always to be other than here,
The self-escapist's single wish.
One resorts to librium, another
To Laing, and the lipping sea sings:
Come south, remember the cargo
Of oranges at Kos, bobbing in the harbour,
Soporiferous swell, swell and swash.
Earth is not your element.
Consider wheeling gull's clamour,
First places, new possibilities,
Sweet sting of fret. This is your fate.

Dark tide turns thoughts,
Opal moon pulls. Only let men
Be not restless, but wrestlers,
Masters. Let them discover home.

Between

Flying over the hyphen ocean,
Such sunlight burns up
Separation, isolation, hermetic insularity.
All our lives are departing and arriving:
This page falls between page and page.
Today I'm in transit
Between my father and my son, indefinite.

One

So we spin. And the seldom best we do
Is some gloss on ourselves, some speculation
That arrests for a moment. That is not nothing.

But the howlers about would obliterate that
And make each meaningless with multiplication.
One for all? Perhaps. All for one? Never.

Petrichor

All day she found substitutes. Then she wept,
Alone; and unable to sleep, she kept
Night watch on the static, neon mausoleum.
But the essence of stone is the smell of rain.

What is he thinking? The cold freezes dreams
In his skull. Wrapped in copies of *Reveille,* he leans
Against the entrance to the Underground.
But the essence of stone is the smell of rain.

String-pullers are usually on strings,
Behind each mask still a man who clings
And almost unheard sings at sunrise, dusk, Christmas.
But the essence of stone is the smell of rain.

I am, thou art, he is, we are all bio-degradable:
Fantastic, offer, sunlit, now, unrepeatable,
Absolutely, yours, lifetime, with this packet.
But the essence of stone is the smell of rain.

Nowhere the desolate hours and acres end;
Yet no natural pattern, no human breakage does not mend
Itself. Everywhere such seeming hopelessness
But the essence of stone is the smell of rain.

Vision

Watch me if you want to.
I'm as shifty as a daddy-long-legs
on a polished pane.
You are where I was
and you will never catch me.

Why do you never tire of me?
Is it simply that I am
always beyond you,
all but undiscernible,
air trembling before rain?

I am your pursuit,
your thirst, your one thought;
only the mirage
that only will refresh you.
Watch me (if you want to).

IV

Glum's Warping

Remember the way west up over Hrafkel's land?
The path string-thin, sorry as a sheep run,
Out of his shieling and into Shut Wood?
Men called that the mossmen's track.
Year after year we used to climb it,
Pairs or small groups strapped with paniers,
Until the troll-terror. . . . True?
Listen to this, and you will not need ask.
See my old hand: with hammer-sign
And sign of cross I swear it so.

Glum Gunnarson ganged up with me.
(He turned many heads, handsome,
Fearless, eager for fame. On his account
Married women wished they were widows
And single girls slept uncertainly.)
It was July. Just after dawn
We met and, chewing mastic, made
Our way through Shut Wood. After that,
A short cut beneath Shouting Cliff
And so we reached the moss rafts under the glacier.

For ten seconds I'd turned my back,
Having a piss. Imagine this:
Glum was straining every sinew, racing
Up towards the glacier; and there, ghastly
On an icy spur, sat a troll-
Woman, waiting. Ugly and gigantic,
With huge, crossed hands she beckoned him.
'Glum! Glum!' I yelled. No good.
He buried himself in her breast without a backward glance
And she loped away over the ice.

THE POETRY BOOK SOCIETY

The Poetry Book Society, founded in 1954, is non-profit-distributing, and receives financial assistance from the Arts Council of Great Britain

---

Membership costs £7.80 (£6.30 for students) per year and brings post free the following:

* A book of new poetry every quarter.

* With the book, the Society's Bulletin with contributions from the authors of the books chosen and recommended.

* A special Poetry Supplement at Christmas. (2 copies)

* A yearly check list of books of new verse.

The Choice

The quarterly book of poetry is chosen for members by Selectors appointed every year by the Society's Board of Management. It is always a book of new poems. During the Society's existence some of the most interesting poetry of the day has come to members on publication.

The Recommendations

The Selectors also recommend, every quarter, any other books of special merit. The recommendations are announced in the Society's Bulletin which also prints specimen poems. In addition to books of new poems, volumes of collected poems and anthologies of contemporary poetry are eligible for recommendation (but not for choice).

Advantages

Since a subscription costs no more than the published price of the books members receive, an obvious benefit is derived from membership. In addition a member knows that the book he receives has been carefully selected by experts, usually practising poets or critics.

It need hardly be said that the Society serves the needs of organisations such as schools (many of which are in membership) as well as those of individuals, since one result of continued membership is the building up of a representative library of the best modern verse.

There are hidden advantages too: the Society's existence certainly encourages publishers to publish books of new poetry and to keep their price to the minimum. To become a member of the Society is a practical way of helping the art and dissemination of poetry.

Poetry Festivals

The Society promotes an annual festival of international poetry each summer in London. Advance details are supplied to all members.

How to join the Society

Either   A   Fill in the Order Form opposite and send with a remittance to the address below

    or   B   Fill in the Banker's Order Form opposite and send it to the address below

The Secretary
The Poetry Book Society Limited
105 Piccadilly
London W1V 0AU

'I have always held firmly that a nation which ceases to produce poetry will in the long run cease to be able to enjoy and even understand the great poetry of its own past.' T. S. ELIOT, O.M.

at a press conference held by the Poetry Book Society, 10 April 1956

---

oetry Book Society   Order Form A

ase enrol me as a member of the Poetry Book Society for *this/next
lendar year at a cost of £7.80 or its equivalent in foreign currency.
or bona fide students the rate is £6.30 or its equivalent in foreign
urrency.

* *Delete as applicable*   My cheque is enclosed/Please send me a bill

Block letters please

Name *(Mr/Mrs/Miss)*_____

Address *(in full)*_____

_____

Date _____

_____

Poetry Book Society   Banker's Order B

To *(name and address of bank)*_____

_____

Please pay to the account of The Poetry Book Society Limited
(A/C Number 46707440) at Messrs Coutts and Company, 440 Strand,
London WC2. (Clearing code 18-00-02)

the sum of_____ due on_____*(date of payment)*

and pay a similar sum on 1 January of each succeeding year until
further notice.

Block letters please

Name *(Mr/Mrs/Miss)*_____

Address *(in full)* _____

_____

Signed _____

Date _____

tear off here

That dear man was mourned in Blafell,
He was missed at the Alithing. People thought
The ogress might rub him with ointment – as one
Rubbed Thorvald thirty years ago –
And stretch him, and shout into his ears,
Trying to turn him into a troll.
And no grey-haired man at all gave Glum
The least chance of escaping the giantess
If he had licked her ladle; they said
His fate would be to fare the fells always.

Summer, autumn, the usual antiphon,
Then the dirge of winter: we lit candles
For Glum, hopeless, yet grim and hoping.
The next spring two shepherds –
I was out from Iceland, south over sea –
They found Glum at the foot of the glacier,
Tatterdemalion. With cries and tears
They greeted him. One asked, 'Are you still man?'
The other: What do you believe in?'
'God,' growled Glum and at once stumped away.

Next summer solstice I saw him myself,
My friend, gruesome, with a growth of hair for clothing.
Savagely he scowled as he shrithed from the glacier;
He was so surly, a fimbul-fambi with no tongue,
And yet he stayed by me – what was he thinking?
Of girls with fair tresses, friendship in Blafell?
'Glum Gunnarson, what do you believe in?'
'Trunt, Trunt,' he grunted. 'Trunt,
And the trolls in the fells.' He guffawed and stalked off,
Gone for ever. That is the end of the story.

* *The rudiments of this poem derive from a story collected by*
Jón Arnason in The Folktales and Fairy Tales of Iceland

Memories of the Gododdin

Three hundred . . .
                                    . . . waves
. . .d gold-torqued they gall . . .
Came to Catraeth . . .
                              . . .bl . . .
                        . . . blue blades . . .
                  . . . staunch . . .
            . . . struck were not struck ag . . .
. . . made wives w . . .
                              . . . grey-haired
. . . ale mead . . .
Stag strong, stronger . . .
                              . . . brunt . . .
And buckler . . .
Crimson . . .   . . . lack crows
Host . . .   . . . ave
And grave . . .
            . . . soaked for my song's sake
                        . . . Catraeth
Three hun . . .
                        . . . three . . .

Namings

1.

Loved one.

Luckless one, Leicester's wife. Did you trip on the
stairs, misery blind, or did some paid hand push you?

You secrete a sweet tuberous root. And George Melly
could gather all the nuts he wants in you.

2.

Dutchman from Groot who became a Scottish landowner.

Much declined in a song.

Son of thunder.

3.

You went west over sea, and fell out with your fellows;
so went on west and did a great publicity job on Greenland.

You swell, little by little. In you a source of sustenance,
second to none, for millions.

4.

A good name for an Amazon, or Grendel's mother: battle-
might.

Not a bit of it. Your name is redolent of moon-faced
poets summoning loved ones into dark gardens, rustle of
crinolines, the baritone with the fruity voice standing
by the upright piano.

You swept Stephen and the swagman into your dance.

5.

Reckless self-conqueror, who lost the world for love.

Often enough you drop an aitch. You're a reckling.

Desert father, reckoned to be the first monastic. Lord
of unlikely places: pig sties and lost property offices.

6.

Sky-blue forget-me-not and love-in-a-mist that's violet;
ashen old man's beard, silver and grey; rose, rose; white
for the arum lily.

These are your initials, a corner of your petalled
kingdom.

7.

A very strange fish: a kind of mini-cod.

Whose pregnant mother dreamed of a dog-son (not a godson)
with black and white spots, firing the world with a
flame.

The Lord's own.

8.

'My sweet girl . . .'

In you a spread of feathers and another name; an old-
fashioned negative and a fairy.

Diminutive of the lady from Rimini.

9.

Eider ducks kept you company, and keep your memory.

Genius of the two fists at Durham, of Great Farne
and Lindisfarne and the girdling flint-grey water.
Becket of the north, miracle-worker.

You embody truth.

10.

I'd have guessed some brownish, Brobdingnagian growth.

White breast, white breast, all points west from Chester,
Gloucester and Shrewsbury.

11.

Link between a King of Cornwall and Samuel L. Clemens.

You score both skin and silver. Men mint you in nickel.

Did you run naked from Gethsemane? As your city sinks,
you record the rising of an everlasting city.

12.

Little bear.

Leader of eleven thousand, all of them virgins, massacred
on sight by the Huns. There's a likely story.

Pattern of stars, with an elder sister.

13.

To sham, to be sceptical, these are your attributes.

But you're half the man you are when it's time for the
M.O.T. It has you in a dither and an awful didymus.

Henry and Richard, they're your blood brothers, under-
ones, men of the streets.

14.

Traveller from Denmark, settler in France, cause of a
song and dance in Sicily.

Roman of the north, beginning where you end, like the
Midgard serpent encircling the earth, biting its own
tail.

In you a norn, shaper of was or is or will be sitting
under the world ash.

15.

Member of the Order of Merit and the Irish Republican
Army.

Fate governing men and godlike men and the gods them-
selves; inescapable and ineluctable from the Stygian
depths to the scree of high Olympus.

16.

One made laws, four fell into two parts and seven
introduced a new line.

Beans meanz heinz; heinz means you.

Your chief defect: chewing little bits of string.

17.

Bagged:

       a brace of indefinite articles;

       an anagrammatic giant panda;

       a four-letter word and a palindrome.

18.

A great man.

Hacked down by the war-wolves; your skull cloven with
an axe and the bones of your body immured in a pillar
in the pink cathedral of Kirkwall.

In you the lamb and the millenium: the first resurrection.

19.

Queen of plums, plumpest Queen.

It was you who rewrote the deservedly little-known
Vita Roci.

Bronze, Maltese, cruciform.

60

20.

Arches over the Vltava (makes a change from waltzes on the Danube).

At first a churl, at last once and future king; but still, an ill-omened name for rulers.

The nicest child I ever knew.

21.

You accommodate several creatures: the nit and the obstinate ram, and the bird zipping through the marram or whistling under the eaves.

Like a third son in a wondertale, you shared what you had: the result, exposure.

Son of the fourth planet.

22.

Who lopped off Holofernes' head; whose father was Charles the Bald; who sat on the marriage see-saw with Esau.

That's enough to be going on with.

23.

Old, white-haired, brainless, and very liable to see the world upside down.

Of Malmesbury, Norwich and Newburgh.

The first one was a bastard and the second red; the next half was red mixed with yellow and the last fathered bastards. (Another one was pink.)

24.

You're fifty, and hairy . . .

You serve a term in the Courts of Law and Learning.

Androgynous, always cheerful.

Answers:

1.	Amy	13.	Thomas
2.	John	14.	Norman
3.	Eric	15.	Moira
4.	Matilda or Maud	16.	Henry
5.	Anthony	17.	Anna
6.	Flora	18.	Magnus
7.	Dominic	19.	Victoria
8.	Fanny	20.	Charles
9.	Cuthbert	21.	Martin
10.	Bronwen	22.	Judith
11.	Mark	23.	William
12.	Ursula	24.	Hilary

Rhyme

Understand rhyme.

Something more than most poets need, fending off the
dangerous random, final, consolation, a sort of friend
at the end of the line.